How Evergreen Kept His Color

Dedicated to all the little humans of the world - Never lose your creativity and imagination.

Once upon a time, in a colorful world, filled with imagination and the power to be yourself, lived a group of magical markers that could bring any drawing to life, creating anything their hearts desired. These markers came in all different shades, from deep blue to bright yellows, and a rainbow trail between, always changing their shapes and colors. Despite their differences, they all shared two important rules amongst themselves - always be yourself and always keep your cap on when not in use.

Among these markers was Evergreen, an adventure seeker who was often so excited, he forgot things. The one thing he often forgot was putting his cap back on after drawing.

One sunny morning, all the markers gathered around a blank piece of paper, ready to create a special masterpiece. With each stroke, their collective imagination brought the paper to life with swirls of color and unique designs.

As the hours passed, the drawing grew bigger and more beautiful. Everyone was so focused on their work, no one was paying attention to what the other markers were doing. No one had their eye on Evergreen or his cap.

The markers were so busy, they didn't realize what time of day it was. One marker friend noticed the sun was beginning to set which meant the end of the day was getting closer.

They decided it was time to clean up, wash up, and get some rest so they could continue their creations in the morning.

As they began cleaning up, Violet noticed Evergreen didn't have his cap. Violet asked him where it was, but Evergreen, as he often did, forgot where he put it.

All the markers frantically started looking for his cap, searching high and low, behind shelves, and underneath tables and chairs, but no one could see it. Throughout the room, you could hear the panic as the markers were running around.

A member of the group, Bianca, asked

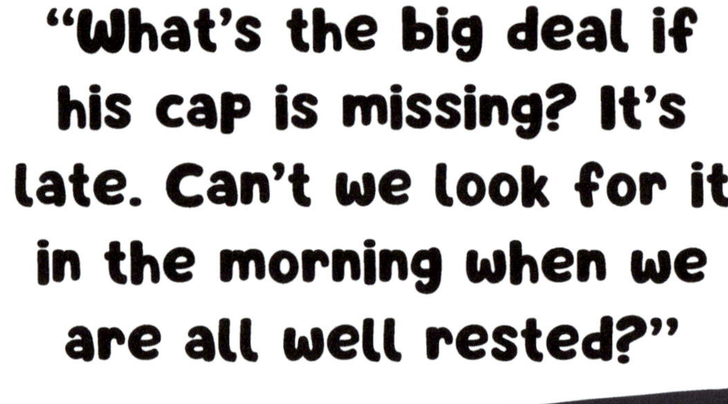

" Without our caps, we will become dry. If we dry up, we cannot color anymore. If Evergreen dries up, how will we create grass and trees? How will our dinosaurs and dragons come to life? What about the frogs and the turtles? If one of us dries up, a part of our magic disappears."

Evergreen frowned. He felt so bad that he caused so much trouble for all of his friends. He was afraid of drying up and he didn't want to let any of his friends down. He took a deep breath and suggested they divide themselves into groups to continue searching. He said each group could take one area of the room to search.

And so everyone took a deep breath, divided themselves into groups, and continued to search. Only this time, it was more organized and a lot calmer.

After a couple of minutes of more searching high and low, Bianca yelled out "Hey everyone! I think I found it!" All the markers ran over and saw underneath the radiator a sliver of green. Bianca reached down, picked the green cap up, and placed it firmly on Evergreen's head.

Evergreen responded by giving her a big hug. He turned to his friends and apologized for being careless and causing a commotion for them all. He thanked them for their help in finding his cap and for not giving up on him. He promised to keep track of his cap from now on.

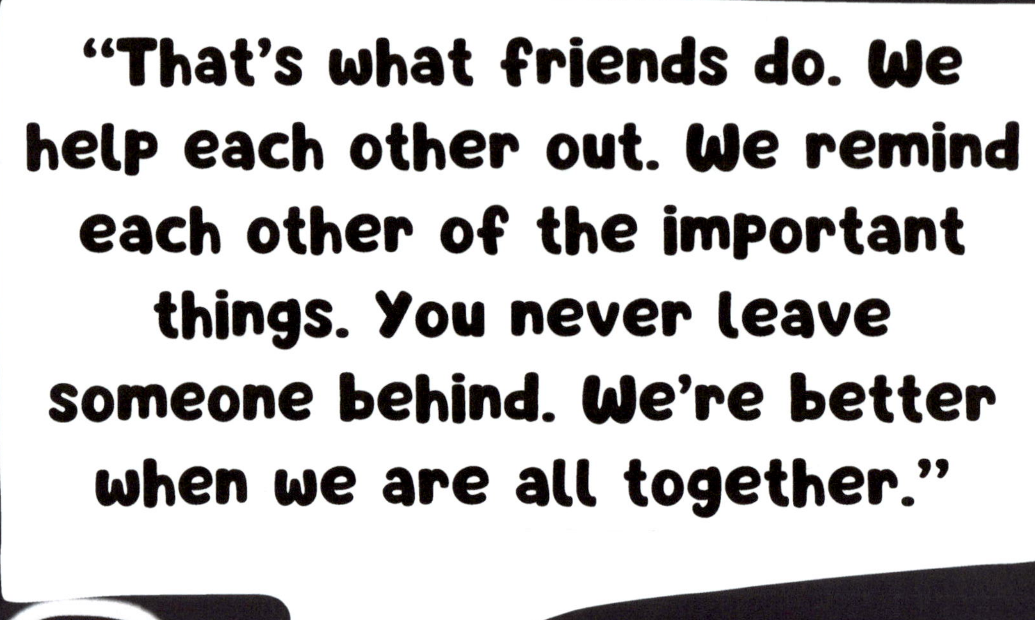
"That's what friends do. We help each other out. We remind each other of the important things. You never leave someone behind. We're better when we are all together."

They all embraced in a large
group hug and then walked back
to their bin to settle in for the
night.

After that night, Evergreen kept his promise and always had his cap close to him and he never forgot to put it on again. He realized having his cap on wasn't just to keep himself safe from drying up, but was also a sign of respect and consideration for his friends.

Whenever any of the marker friends looked at Evergreen and his cap, they were reminded of the importance of taking care of themselves, taking care of each other, and taking care of the world around them.

And so with their caps in hand, Evergreen and his marker friends continued to fill the world with their colorful creations, spreading magic, inspiration, and joy wherever they went, knowing that together, they were unstoppable.

And they all inspired creatively
ever after.